the

drowning

room

the drowning room

poems by

damien shuck

newamericanpress

Milwaukee, Wis. • Urbana, Ill.

newamericanpress

www.NewAmericanPress.com

© 2013 by Damien Shuck

All rights reserved. No part of this publication may be reproduced, stored in a retrieval system, or transmitted, in any form or by any means, electronic, mechanical, photocopying, recording, or otherwise, without the prior written permission of the copyright holder.

Printed in the United States of America

ISBN 978-1-9415610-0-3

Book design by David Bowen

For ordering information, please contact:
Ingram Book Group
One Ingram Blvd.
La Vergne, TN 37086
(800) 937-8000
orders@ingrambook.com

TABLE OF CONTENTS

One Summer	11
J Was a Psycho Meth Addict	13
Optimists Just Plan on Sunshine	15
A Murder of Crows	16
Smoker	18
Employee Orientation: You and Your Machine	20
What a Friend Is	23
If I Am Ever Famous Enough to be Asked If I Have Any Advice for Young Poets	25
Yogurt Race	27
Trial Drug Testing Opportunities Available	29
Creation	31
This Is Me	33
The Right Kind of Fishermen	36
Let's Start with the Eyes	37
36 Hours to Live	39

The Last Words	42
Story Involving Porpoise	43
Paid for by Union Carbide a Subsidiary of Dow Chemical	45
In Kathleen's Head	49
Caught in an Argument between Christian and Atheist Friends, Both of Whom Are Way Too Invested, I am Asked if There Is a God	52
Career Outlook for Aspiring Mountains	55
Your New Career	57
Williams' Plums	59
To Friends in New England	60
Ways to Tell You're in Dublin	62
Why Poetry?	63
Evolution	65
A Plea for Leniency	67
Dogs I Owned in a Dream I Had	69
How Water Protects Us	72
Kate Poems	74
An Entirely True Story	77

Spring Chores	79
We'll Need a Cartoon Mascot	81
A Little Service Please	83
Ignorance Always Thinks It Knows Best Because It Doesn't Know Any Better	85
Before The War of the Asphodels	87
What I Got	90
My Cancer Hogs the Covers	93
To Devan's Daughter	95

I am so wise I had my mouth sewn shut.

— John Berryman

One Summer

V lived in a big house a few blocks over.
Her dad put on "Lime in the Coconut"
while we tripped acid. He used to tell her
her boobs were growing in good.
Tried to get the sixteen-year-old girls
to sit on his lap. Another time at V's house
I lay under the dartboard staring up
at the five hundred wobbly, singing darts
following the first into the board.
I recommend this to no one.
After V lit the house on fire
with a half-full bottle of grain alcohol
and an aroma therapy candle, we called her
Sparky. That whole summer
she was on house arrest. Her dad moved
her to the basement and put a lock on her door
but not her window so she would sneak
out to the front yard to smoke a cigarette.
I would pick her up
and throw her out of the yard
to try to set off her ankle bracelet.
After the first month of hard sobriety
she stuck an orange under her mattress.
She had heard that if you eat the mold you can

get high. She tried to eat it and threw up
on her beanbag chair; I started calling her
Nasty or Sparky, depending on my mood.
After that summer none of us saw her much.
Heard she got into meth, had a kid
with her dealer. But I can see her spin
in small circles, press her fingers
into the sky. Dance between cinders
to the music of distant sirens.
Blow smoke rings at God.

J Was a Psycho Meth Addict

asshole. So it was not a real loss
when the police planted six bullets in his chest
to see what would grow. Nothing,
because these are lead bullets and not seeds
but I think seeds would make really good bullets.
When someone is buried they would have their own tree
to be buried under. They would have their own
flowers so in case anyone forgot
to bring some they could just say they threw in
on those flowers, who's going to argue?
But this poem isn't about J
who I have said was a psycho
meth addict asshole and he did point his pistol
at the police first, and you have to expect that
sort of abrupt end.

It happened the same weekend as the buffalo
which is the reason I bring it up.
They were blocking traffic
and eating a few lawns.
When the cops showed up a few hours later,
they just stood in a line, pistols out.
They got to be cowboys for the day.
The young buffalo in their red jackets

on one side of the street. Coppers
on the other, dropping copper jackets.
Police Shoot Up Town To Stop Livestock.

They fired 125 rounds, mostly into houses,
mailboxes, shrubs –about thirty
entered buffalo. Small caliber gnats,
but they were everywhere, and they were enough,
finally. The buffalo didn't build a meth lab
next to a day care. I would bet that the buffalo
did not fire first, or possess crack at the time.
But the cops still made all the appropriate
buffalo killing whoops and hollers,
the kind that used to be heard a lot.

Optimists Just Plan on Sunshine

Pessimists invent the umbrella.

Optimists are sure they will recover.

Pessimists invent medicine.

Optimists invented PR

because they were sure everyone wanted to know them.

Optimists invented the picnic,

which forced pessimists to invent tarps, gazebos, bug spray,

sun block, hand sanitizer and bear mace. Optimists invented television

because they never saw reality TV coming.

Optimists invented the computer,

so pessimists invented virus protection software and back-up files

because we were sure that their invention would lose all our stuff.

Pessimists also created an entire law enforcement section

to counter the child pornography that we were positive

their invention would proliferate.

In 1861 optimist Dr. Robert Gatling invented a gun

he said was so devastating

that it would put an end to all war forever.

Eighty years later optimists said the same thing when

they invented the nuclear bomb.

A Murder of Crows

Crows are tired of being hungry. Entrepreneurial in nature, they realize that there are plenty of live squirrels in forests near fresh nuts. These squirrels are no good to them since they are still the living variety of squirrel, and crows are only interested in the dead variety. But they also realize that there are a disproportionately large number of dead squirrels on the hard black rivers which run through the countryside. Why, they think, do we not bring the nuts, and thus the live variety of squirrel to the road, where they can be processed into the dead? Besides, crows like hanging around the roads anyway; the roads are their favorite color. So they start to drop nuts onto the roads. This works well.

But the crows are still hungry. Not all the squirrels that they lure onto the road are killed quickly enough. We need more of these loud zoomy cows. The new head of research and development says, Cars. So the crows start their own tourist trap to lure more cars, to kill more squirrels. The sign on the interstate says, World's Largest Road Kill Collection. Stop On In. It is very popular with tourists because it is so interactive.

But the crows are still hungry. So the crows need more nuts, more squirrels and more cars. The nuts are now imported from Panama at a very fair rate per metric ton. The squirrels are taking care of themselves after some slight genetic modification. But crows still need more cars. Research and development comes back with news that cars eat oil. More oil, more cars. So the crows, now called Crow Inc. begins to import oil. They like oil, it is their favorite color. But there are people living over the oil. These people believe that it is their oil, not Crow Inc. oil. Something has to be done, and quickly, before Crow Inc. output drops and they start to disappoint their stockholders. So Crow Inc. gets into the business of armament design and construction to make weapons to kill the people, to keep the oil, to fuel the cars, to kill the squirrels so that the crows can stop being hungry.

Hal is hired to fly his plane around and drop sandwiches and box lunches onto roads where the oil people live. For this he is paid astronomical amounts of money and all the free squirrel carcasses he can eat. After Hal finishes the food drops to lure the people onto the roads, another large, black, carrion bird, which research and development calls a Solution Delivery System, drops bombs. After many years of this, Crow Inc. decides to further diversify, to stop eating squirrel entirely. There are plenty of other carcasses lying around by now, burnt black, their favorite color.

Smoker

She smoked a cigarette like Marilyn Monroe. Would wet each lip, then press them forward to meet the tip, like a kiss in the backseat of a Cadillac in 1962.

She said, used to be a dancer, and I believed in every line of her body. In the way she walked, each glass foot placed precisely, like she was afraid of breaking the ground, like glass, glass, glass, surrounded her.

She wore the same faded gray sweatshirt, with the same hole in the sleeve she stuck the same nail-bitten thumb through. The same faded blue jeans, with the same henna patterns in the same faded gray ink.

She wasn't perfect.

She needed someone to tell her to pluck her eyebrows; they were like a herd of water buffalo migrating across the plain of her forehead.

She would joke that she would cut strips of flesh from her thighs.

She'd say, ten more pounds or I'll never be pretty.

She was beautiful.

She moved to the coast, began to sell it for coke, wanted to break into porn films.

She told me once, if you give me a cigarette, I'll love you forever.

I rolled one down my fingers, down the table.

I said, that's my line.

EMPLOYEE ORIENTATION: YOU AND YOUR MACHINE

- The machine must be serviced every day.
- You will turn on the machine at six o'clock every morning, seven days a week.
- You will turn off the machine at eleven o'clock every night, seven days a week.
- You will service the machine every day of the year.
- You will be responsible for servicing the machine on holidays.
- You will have to arrange any days off or sick days with other employees assigned to service the machine.*
- You will hurry.
- You will be back in time for your normal work hours.
- You will not allow your duties to the machine to interfere with your normal work hours.

*You are the only employee currently assigned to service the machine.

- You will drive miles out of your way to reach the machine.
- You will furnish your own car.
- You will furnish your own car insurance.
- You will have the opportunity to attend a safe driving course.*

* The safe driving course will be mandatory.

- When you are not at work or servicing the machine you will be on-call to service the machine should an error occur.
- You will be responsible for repairing any errors the machine has.
- Any errors can be fixed by reading the manual.*

*You do not have the authority to read the manual.**

You may submit a written request to see the manual.*

***Per article seven, section eight of the manual, "All requests to see the manual will be denied."

- You may apply to be reimbursed for fifteen percent of the total cost of the safe driving course.*
- You will receive no additional monetary reimbursement for your commute.
- You will not be paid for the time spent on your commute.
- You will only be paid for the time you actually work on the machine.
- You will receive no additional monetary compensation for working on holidays.
- You will receive no additional monetary compensation for being on call.
- You will receive no additional monetary compensation for the time you work on the machine.
- You will receive an additional 3-4 hours of work at your normal pay grade for the time actually spent working on the machine which should amount to no more than twenty-one additional dollars per week.

- Any time spent on the machine totaling more than twenty-one dollars a week will be deducted from your normal work hours.

*Reimbursement is contingent upon an audit by the oversight management committee determining adequate availability of funds.**

**The oversight management committee has determined there are no available funds.

- Failure to attend or pass the safe driving course may result in immediate termination.
- Any failure to meet your normal work hours for the week may result in immediate termination.
- Any failure to furnish a replacement from the available pool of employees currently assigned to service the machine may result in immediate termination.
- Any requests for days off or sick days must be requested at least six days in advance in order to receive approval from the oversight management committee.
- Failure to receive approval may result in immediate termination
- As per article eight, section seven, of the manual, "Any request to see the manual may be viewed as a sign of incompetence on the part of the employee and may result in immediate termination."
- Any failure in the performance of any of your normally assigned duties or any duties relating to the machine or any failings of the machine in your absence may result in a probation hearing with the oversight management committee which will result in immediate termination.

What a Friend Is

Once they learned that sex burns
more calories than hiking, Stacey and Dave
changed their workout routine and started dating.
A metaphor comes to mind of two ships in the night
which run headlong into each other,
poison thousands of oblivious penguins.

When the three of us go to dinner
there is now a my side of the table, a theirs.
A silence every once in a while,
while they stop, look at each other.
I tell them how poetry is a coke machine. How I agree
the second person to compare a rose to a lover was an idiot.
How frost on cherry blossoms isn't really a metaphor
for anything, except a shortage of cherries.
But a shortage of cherries is an excellent metaphor
for our old high school. I tell them the etymology
of the word amok, as in running amok,
a story deeply rooted in feces, just like everything else.

Then one night she says she is pregnant.

His response to her,

"I hope we can still be friends." That is what a friend is.

Someone you don't punch in the face.

Even though you really, really want to.

If I Am Ever Famous Enough to be Asked If I Have Any Advice for Young Poets

Jane says that a poem is a coke machine.
Put a quarter in, scream
and pound your fists until you tip it over,
get crushed to death, maybe win a Darwin Award.
That bad poets fall in love with themselves.
That good poets fall in love with everything else.
That poetry is the economy of loss.

I say all poets should drive a stolen car
at least once, in order to know how
power steering works.
That all poets bleed internally, probably
from a microscopic crack in the left ventricle.
A way of saying broken heart.
You can't say broken heart.
Out of the two thousand gallons of blood
the heart pumps in one day,
some is bound to be lost in transit.
It won't kill you
to be a poet but then again, statistically, it might.

I say all poets should be on drugs.
Then be off drugs. Then write

about the cool stuff they did when they were high.
That you will never escape now,
even when you are hidden beneath the covers,
poetry is crouched in your room,
eyes never resting, clutching a big knife.

Jane says believe. That if you are ever stuck,
get out of your head. But, if you have no idea
what that means, or if your head is encased
in some calcified cage, get back in the car,
get the fuck out of town.

Yogurt Race

On my way back from the grocery store
a car pulls up next to me
with four nineteen-year-olds, one leans out his window
and yells, "We're drunk."
And I believed him since he did display some signs of intoxication,
such as screaming "We're drunk," at strangers.
Then they rev their engine and the one from before yells,
"Let's go man let's go." So I tear off at the green light.
Their car is old and a little crappy but my car,
while not a sports car, is at least new and in good shape.

I whiz past and think about what would happen if I keep going.
Leave their car two smiling eyes in the rearview
that disappear in the distance like a wave goodbye.
Then I could see how far I can go before the cops
get a tire strip in front of me and pull me from the car.

But I hit 50 mph, 5 over the speed limit
and I slow down. I don't need another ticket
and I can't afford for my insurance to go up
and it probably won't help me get tenure
if I am on America's Craziest Police Chases
so I slow down.

Here the other car's one advantage,
driven by drunk teenagers,
takes hold and they pass me.
When we get to the red light up ahead,
I tell them "good job, you won."
I toss through their window a yogurt I just bought
and say not to waste it.

Trial Drug Testing Opportunities Available

If you're not happy
with your current birth control,
try new PLACEBO brand oral contraceptive.
This breakthrough technology
was first pioneered in the 1950's
in our state-of-the-art medical research center
in beautiful Rio Piedras, Puerto Rico.
However, despite extensive testing,
this revolutionary new pill
has only recently become available in the United States.
The amazing proprietary technology in PLACEBO
contains no progesterone and no estrogen,
synthetic or otherwise. Like you need any more of that,
am I right ladies? No initial side effects.
PLACEBO is available in mint or orange flavors.
Only one calorie per serving.
Finally an oral contraceptive
with all the miraculous powers of placebo.

Placebo is for the prevention of pregnancy.
Try it now, recommend it to a friend,
don't recommend it simply replace their pills
with new PLACEBO. Trust me, they will thank you.
PLACEBO birth control pills are the only

oral contraceptive available
without a prescription.
So try PLACEBO brand birth control pills today.

Warning: Do not take Thalidomide while using Placebo
as serious complications may occur.
Placebo is ineffective in treating acne.
Severe side effects were reported between 1-9 months
by women after taking Placebo
including but not limited to:
Severe weight gain, nausea, vomiting,
morning sickness accompanied by vomiting,
swollen ankles, uncontrollable appetite,
bizarre food cravings, mood swings,
hormone imbalances, severe weight gain,
abdominal swelling, cramping,
years of insomnia and inability to sleep
through the night, uncontrollable lactating,
swelling of mammary glands (you're welcome),
Back and/or joint pain, constipation, acid reflux,
hemorrhoids and unexplained movement in the abdomen.
Do not take PLACEBO to prevent pregnancy
if you run the risk of pregnancy or could become pregnant.

CREATION

It was all suddenly there,
ficus, monkey puzzle tree,
monkeys to be puzzled,
macaws and macaques,
mangroves and mangoes,
mountains and my personal favorite,
the tarsier, an alien/bat/owl/lemur hybrid.

All the peoples of earth
more or less, just suddenly there.
Eating mangoes and coconuts, the occasional
small mammal, collecting pretty rocks.
You just knew.

Before the end of the seventh day,
two o'clock, fighting had broken out.
The day before, God
had created the apple.
There was only one apple though.
Everybody wanted it.
He had invented want.

What was a clearing with homes
made mostly of palm leaves was split

into camps. We invented the fence,
ditches filled with water
you were yelled at for swimming in.

We sharpened the first stick
and lifted the first rock
over the head of the first victim.
All for the first apple.
A week after, He made one grape.

Maybe next week, a pickle.

This Is Me

> From *A History of Violence*

You think it is hard giving birth.
Try giving birth to yourself, but a new you.
That is the emotional crap, ya know, sounds deep, right?
Yea, I read a book once too ya know? Really
it was a lot of hard work.

> I tried. I thought he was gone.
> That was just a lie though.

Changing your accent is hard work.
It gets easier after a while, but not one slip in years,
that takes perse-fuckin-verance.

> At one of my son's baseball games,
> some jerk was yelling at the kids,
> and I told him to relax, it's just kids, let them play.
> The guy stood up and turned around. Told me to mind my own business,
> why don't I leave before something happens. And I saw Joey.

The hardest part, being a pussy cat
all the time, backing down.

How many times in the course of a week you run
across someone who deserves to get their throat cut ya know?

> I saw Joey punch him right in the throat,
> push him over backwards, off the bleachers.
> I saw Joey jump down, both legs straight into this guy's chest.
> Woulda broke a couple ribs at least.
> I just said, sorry fella, my mistake, let's just enjoy the day all right?
> If it weren't for those two guys in the diner.

Those two no account backwater rats.
They weren't tough guys. I've known tough guys and those two weren't.
They were just a couple of assholes, ya know? A real bad element.
You ask me? They're better off that way. Did a public service.

> I thought that maybe it was me. Maybe I killed those two. Self-defense.
> Instinct took over. I still had some things in my head
> from Joey, what to do. But I knew different. I couldn't do those things.
> I really knew he was back when he looked out the window
> and knew that reporters don't hang around in funeral black Lincolns.
> But I knew who did.

> It is hard not being Joey. It is hard to love my son

instead of slapping him across his smart mouth.
These kids, they got no respect for nothing.

This is me.

    This is me asking my wife for…

So I killed a few people. So what? What's the big deal? It's not like she knew any of them.

    This is me, washing Joey away.

The Right Kind of Fishermen

My father and brother are fish gods.
Their lines connect them
to the water, stretched tight.
Drops of it cling to the thread.
Eyes squinted, hands intent, they cast.

The story of my fishing is a series of snag,
knot in line, hook beneath fingernail, snag,
reel somehow falls off pole and rolls into stream,
a trajectory hook impeded in nipple, snag.

I have not caught a fish in years.
I say I lack the right beat in my chest.
Fish like something they can dance to.
I'm told I give up too easy, that I'm impatient.
My brother adds that I am stupid.

But my father and brother are the right kind of fishermen,
blonde. They stand at the very edge of the water, touch it
delicately with their lines. And the fish offer themselves
as if they had dreamt of a heaven their whole lives.
A heaven where they can't even breathe.

Let's Start with the Eyes

Should be easy, Two tiny moons flee predator
by escaping into deeper waters? Close.
The pale shark gaining on them, a flash of teeth?
No. The shark we will have to save,
the one living in your hips, for the way you move
without displacing the air.
Your breasts like a symphony
composed entirely by orchids and coral,
but the pretty coral, not the stuff that looks like brains.

Your neck, a number of animal comparisons
spring to mind but you are almost,
but not quite, exactly different than a swan.
And a giraffe seems mildly insulting,
though your tongue may be bruised purple
from the constant stream of curse words you use as punctuation.
Fresh milk mozzarella? Rhubarb? Back to the eyes.
Plums, perhaps. So sweet and so cold.
You see how hard this is. Especially since, for a poet,
I am incredibly shallow.

But for a twenty-seven-year-old man
I am remarkably well preserved.
Due I am sure to this hand lotion

which was sent to me by a mysterious Norwegian fisherman
and which I am convinced is made largely of whale urine
but does prevent cracks and remarkably,
cures warts on your hands
but since it is not made by an actual company
and I do not know the name of the fisherman,
you will have to find a whale and squeeze your own.
Which brings me to the point of this poem
which is actually an advertisement
for scuba gear. Scuba gear which was left at my house
and which I will sell to you
for the very reasonable price of one kiss.
The money for the oxygen in the tank
we can discuss after we're under water.

36 Hours to Live

If you had a little longer, maybe plan a sky diving trip.
Climb a mountain. 36 hours really isn't enough time.
Go with the basics. I would smoke 3 packs or so.
I'd light them with a Zippo for that smooth roll
of the wheel under your fingers, and the smell.

It would be tempting to get drugged up.
Some acid, some mushrooms, sit around
and drink, smoke pot, try to find opiate derivatives.
I don't know. Could be fun but I'm not sure I would
want to spend my last 36 hours all fucked up.
If I had 2 weeks to live I would
definitely spend at least 5 days screwed out
of my miserable mind. So messed up I could forget
I had just 2 weeks left. But with only 36 hours,
no drugs probably.

On the practical side I would probably call around,
find out where student loans go when you die.
Would my family be responsible? If not,
if they just disappear then shit, I will spend every dime I have.
If my family is responsible for those loans, then I would feel
bad, as I spent every dime. Maybe I'd rob a bank.
Probably wouldn't get enough to pay off

my student loans but it would be a start. I would
definitely rob a bank, probably several. Then a massage.

I would be tempted to spend my time left with my family.
But I am not good at these emotional hugging moments.
We would probably just depress each other.
So I would spend 2 hours getting a massage, and 10 hours
with my family so they don't think I'm a jerk. That is 24 hours left.
Screw my friends. Those jerks. It is probably their fault
I'm in this mess in the first place. They probably gave me something.

I would get into a fist fight. I want that flash of white,
the first time knuckles connect with my nose. I want
my knuckles to hurt. I want to punch someone. I want
to go swimming. I want to float around in lazy circles.
I want to hold my head under.

I might want to sleep. I do love sleeping. But this seems wasteful.
I would want a real hamburger. I know a place that serves them
the size of your head, just the right amount of grease, cooked
to perfection, slightly crisp on the edges of the patty. I want
a tall, cold glass of water. There is no better taste than cold,
clean water. And I want to drink it in long slow gulps,
letting my mouth fill up before swallowing.
I want to remember that glass of water while I can.
I want to dribble it down my chin. I'd still have some time to kill.

I won't have time for a novel. I may read a few of my favorite poems.
I would miss these. Maybe I'd write a poem. Maybe I'd write
this poem. But I won't write anything, no time to edit later
so what's the point? I hope I don't watch any TV.
I'd lie on the lawn; look up into the gentle sky, reading poetry,
sipping a nice glass of scotch. Smoke like I didn't have to
worry about lung cancer. Perfect. Just lie there
and think. How much time left? 14 hours. Crap. Now what?
Only 14 hours left and nothing to do. This will take forever.
I guess I'd just wait. Play some video games with my brother.
Maybe I will sleep for a while. Watch some TV.

The Last Words

I once saw a man
roll up his sleeves,
flush the urinal
with his elbow;
then wash his hands
but not his elbow.

Story Involving Porpoise

I will tell a story of poems on a boat.
What kind of boat, the young poet asks.
A rowboat.
Can it be a schooner? the young poet asks.
I really hate you sometimes you know.
One poem dips its toe in the water, says
look how brave I am.
Do poems have toes? the young poet asks.
Shut up.
Another scoops a handful of sea
splashes water on his face shouts look
how brave I am, I am far braver than you
to have gotten this wet.

You want to write the poem that leaps
clear of the gangplank
covered in fish blood, lashes itself
to a porpoise and beats it with a shoe
to make it run for its life into deeper waters.
This poem doesn't say shit but gives
the whole boat the finger as it disappears
beneath the beautiful blue and tries its hardest
to drown before reappearing translated into Japanese.

How do I get published? the young poet asks.

When you are building
a reputation you don't want
to serve lamb for dinner, but lion.
It may not taste as good but it proves
what a tough sonofabitch you are.

What is a poem, the young poet asks.

Dobyns defined it as "a small machine
out of words that re-creates the same feeling
in another human being, any time, any place."
But this invites questions.
I say it is a wind-up bird.
Then flap my arms and walk quickly away.

Paid for by Union Carbide a Subsidiary of Dow Chemical

Don't worry.

The billowing cloud of poisonous gas

is not your enemy.

It doesn't even know you

and even if it did

I assure you it will bear no particular grudge

against your race, religion or socio-economic background.

That's nice right?

Do not run

from the billowing cloud of poisonous gas

this will just excite it.

It is best to simply lie down and play dead. Likely,

you will not have to play for very long.

The billowing cloud of poisonous gas

Does not mean any harm. It is just afraid of the dark.

That is why it slipped the leash at Bhopal

and came to look, at midnight, for you.

Picture it. Would a breed help?

Does knowing it is methyl -isocyanate

help you to picture a Bassett hound?

Slow, low to the ground, picture it?

Picture it clawing at the base of your bedroom door.
Picture it begging to be let in because it hears
your breath, in, out, and it just wants to be near you.
Maybe curl up in your lap like a puppy.

And maybe you could fall asleep
while you rub the tips of your fingers along
the cloud's warm, smooth belly.
And in the morning maybe it would press its furry muzzle
into the side of your neck and lick and lick and lick.
And worry why you won't wake up.

> *...they shot her nephew,*
> *nine years old, for stealing a chair. You see he had it wrong.*
> *He should have destroyed the chair.*
>
> — Lynda Hull

In Kathleen's Head

The bird will be ok.
It just has a broken leg.
She will sprinkle
some bird seed in front of it.
Place a small dish of water.
The bird will feel better,
drag itself to the shade.
Kathleen will come back later
with a shoe box she fills with cotton
fibers she pulled and pulled apart
from the bag of cotton balls
in the cabinet next to the sink
in the bathroom with the blue paint
and the drawing of the moose
at the end of the hall upstairs.
Kathleen will put the bird in the shoe box
where it will sit quietly and maybe sleep
in the dark, soft nest Kathleen makes.
Ryan will let the bird in his truck
as he drives her home.
Kathleen will peek at the bird to make sure
the bird is ok and caress the feathers on the back of its neck
with the barest tips of her fingers so lightly
that she could not really be said to have touched them at all

before she leaves it in the garage and goes to bed.
Kathleen will take the box to a veterinarian she knows.
This vet, Susan, will have a soft spot,
a special love of small birds and will agree to take a look.
The bird will just need a splint on its leg
and a long rest and someone to keep it fed.
To give it water. In a few weeks
the bird will be better and Kathleen will let it go
in the park where Brad once caught his jeans on fire
while standing in the coals from our barbeque.
The bird will fly into the trees
and there will be a flock of birds breaking
into sudden motion and sound like a crowd of children
and they will welcome Kathleen's bird
into their frantic cloud before they all head deeper
into the forest toward the lake.
All Kathleen's friends will be there to see it.
We will play Frisbee and eat a few hot dogs
and I will tell the story about Brad
catching his jeans on fire and we will laugh
when I act it out and someone else
will tell a story and then someone else
before we all drive home at sunset feeling good.
Because in Kathleen's head
there is some force in the world that cares
about little birds and wants them to be ok.
But what really happens,

when Kathleen walks inside,

is that the little bird starts convulsing. It looks to be in pain

and since the world does not usually reconcile

what it should be and what we have.

The kind thing, on that day

the caring thing, the thing that will happen,

happens. I hold the bird down and with two fingers and thumb

twist its head around.

Caught in an Argument between Christian and Atheist Friends, Both of Whom Are Way Too Invested, I Am Asked if There Is a God

There is a twelve year old girl right now in a basement.
She is crying. A grown man is pressing down on her,
he took off her clothes. In two days he will get scared and kill her.
Before leaving her body under some leaves
in a forest three hours drive north-west
of the suburb she was kidnapped in.
Two days is a long time.

There is an eight year old boy,
his mother beat him with a chain dog-leash
before locking him in the closet.
She said he had been sneaking cookies.
She said she won't raise a thief.
He didn't take any cookies.
He hasn't been fed in three days.
He would cry but he doesn't have enough water left.
It will take another eighteen hours before
Dehydration kills him.
Eighteen hours is a long time.

There is a woman, nineteen years old.
She is lying on her back on a dirt floor

in the hut she shared with her husband
until eight minutes ago
when she watched as the Janjaweed shot him in the head.
Four men dragged her into this hut.
She was pregnant
until one of the soldiers pulled out a long knife
and dug into her belly
until he could pull out her baby.
It is lying on the floor a few feet to the left of her
and she has turned her head to look at it.
She doesn't want to look down
at the cat that the Janjaweed are just now
stuffing into the cut they had made.
After they sew her stomach closed
they will laugh as they leave.
The cat will not quite make it out
before suffocating. The young woman will live
for three minutes longer than the cat.
Three minutes is a long time.

There is a woman laying face down on a ceramic floor.
Her husband has her arms pinned to her sides with his knees.
It isn't necessary, she had stopped struggling already.
He has his hands clamped to her head
and raises it up just long enough
to slam it down on the tile again.
He will stop in thirteen seconds.

She will be dead in eight.

Eight seconds is a long time.

They will all pray

for God to help them.

So why ask the question?

What difference could it make?

Career Outlook for Aspiring Mountains

Like everyone, you originally wanted to be a mountain
but you slept in late on the day everyone took the mountain test
so that was out. Then you, like everyone
who didn't get to be a mountain, decided you wanted to be a cliff,
which is pretty sweet, you have very little demands on your time
except posing for the occasional picture where you strain
to look dignified but somewhat wistful. And it is an exciting job,
you occasionally get a widow whose husband is lost at sea
or the occasional poet to pay you a surprisingly short visit
on their way to the water below you.
You wish they would stay longer.
But cliff jobs are really hard to get. Super competitive
and you are not really sure of how to look for one
so you think you could be a valley.
You would make an undeniably good valley, and you could
pursue what you have recently decided is a love of goats.
They could spend the day running up and down you
and eat grass out of your various crevassai or crevasses?
Or crevāssia? You should ask somebody about that
so you can sound like you know what you are talking about in the interview.
But you spent your time in college learning how to be a cliff
and never did the valley internship which is kind of a prerequisite to be a valley.
In fact, you read somewhere that companies save around 12 billion dollars a year
in unpaid internships, people working for free

in order to maybe get a job as a valley in the future
and you can't afford to do a year of unpaid valley work
even though you are sure you would make a good valley
and many of your cliff skills would be transferrable.
So you take a gig as a hillock which, let's face it is beneath you
and the pay is terrible but there are worse jobs.
And you still hope to one day be a cliff, maybe you could be a cliff
overseas for a little while. Would that help you get cliff work later?
Is there a way to volunteer to do cliff work in your spare time, will that help?
Everyone tells you to just keep trying. Everyone tells you that
you have plenty of time, that you are still young
until the time no one tells you that anymore.

Your New Career

The secret to dressing for an interview is to iron your pants
into a perfect crease, forget the jacket. Spend a lot of time
on your tie. The knot should be perfect. Wear a nice shirt.
Do not tuck it in. You want to look young.
Let the bastards know that you are not going to take anything
seriously. Explain that the civilized never see their shadow
aimed west. When asked if you have ever had a problem
with a coworker and how it was resolved tell them
about the girl at your last job. The one who always smelled
like pickles. I mean always. To resolve this you kept mints
and held your breath whenever she talked to you.
So maybe you're not brilliant but your shoes sure are.

So you got the job, now you need a day off. Call your boss,
explain that a fire truck and an ambulance block your driveway,
you can't make it in until the old man next door dies.
When you return the next day your boss will ask why
you didn't come in. Just say, "Old guy was a fighter." Then vamoose
to your desk. Your boss will hate you but won't do shit.

When you have to quit, just move, move out of the country.
This is the perfect time
to max out your credit cards with cash advances
and a first class ticket to Ecuador. There is no way your loan

holders or creditors will find you since you are now living perfectly
happy as a beach comber, with no phone or computer,
but all the free shell fish and papaya you can eat.
Just bring sunscreen and some sort of trowel.

You will leave in your cubicle, hands taped to the keyboard,
a blowup doll. It may take months but someone will finally catch on
when a member of HR comes by to promote you
for no longer taking lunch breaks. Take this time to learn a new career,
lobster diving, splitting coconuts for mixed drinks.
Gain the world record for holding your breath. Then hold it professionally,
sell tickets for people to watch you hold your breath to music.
Start your own career advisor service. You are well qualified.

Williams' Plums

He does not say, My tongue
tasted upon that very deed
of pleasure, oh noble plumbe
distilled of the sylvan
spirits of frost which whiten
the wintery whorls
of the north and sweetened by that
self same ambrosial nectar
of our blind poet's gods.
No, he says they were delicious,
so sweet and so cold.
And I don't even like
plums, but I'd buy
a crate of them right now.

To Friends in New England

Then I catch a line, what is a tree in space?
What is the tree doing in space what kind of tree
is it a palm tree all long rocket with green fire
at the top a willow orbited by its tutu how tall is it
when will it get here when it gets here can I climb it
is it poisonous in any way maybe someone else
should climb it first does it still do photosynthesis?
But it is a poem about practical feng shui.
It is how to position a tree in the space from all the walls
and furniture, not outer space at all
but the walls seem to be a metaphor for divorce or
something. The next reader starts, I sing the praises of teeth,
and I think furiously of puppies to hold it together.
The most interesting poem of the night is one by a young woman
called "She is Going Crazy Alphabetically." But she
only writes about A-C then skips to S then ends on W.
I want to tell her to keep going. There are a lot of crazy letters,
Q for instance, but she is already gone. I was not
really interested in this reading but out here I make it
to whatever readings I can. The next poet
walks to the podium wearing a red leather jacket
with tassel fringe along the arms. I envy my poet
friends in New England for not being here, for never
attending a poetry reading where a woman

in a red leather jacket, with tassel fringe along the arms,
zipped all the way to the top in eighty-four degree heat,
reads her poem about a rooster, affecting a fake,
down-home, wild-west accent. Reading her poem
about how mean, I mean, cantankerous the rooster is,
how she eventually eats it. Colorado is where
the west crawled like an old dog, to die.

Ways to Tell You're in Dublin

Even the graffiti is friendly.
Everyone knows more than you do about the American electoral process.
Outside of Connolly Station is a pub named
after a poem you can read if you ask the German bartender nicely.
Everyone is drinking Heineken or Bud Light.
Every third dustbin, wastebasket, trashcan has an umbrella
sticking out like a flag of surrender.
You can order fajita and chips, so too lasagna and chips.
Turns out you love blood pudding.
You can use the bus schedule as an excuse to talk
to beautiful women.
Everywhere is full of beautiful women.
Everywhere is palm trees.
Someone will tell you there are seals about, but this is so far unconfirmed.
The sky is a bowl recently used to smother a fire.
The 31C bus runs four minutes late, which is fine because you missed the
first
six buses while drinking Guinness and reading the poem in the pub
whose name you forgot but is across the street from Connolly Station.
You're home lad, you're home.

Why Poetry?

Perhaps it is my short attention span and impatience.
That I always want to skip to the end, to the good parts.
That I don't have the patience
to describe the color of the table that he is sitting at.
That I don't want to describe what he had for breakfast,
pancakes. That he liked a light amount of syrup
but it was warmed up and came out of the decanter too fast,
went everywhere. That he then tried to eat
around the edge of the pancakes quickly
before the flow of syrup could reach it.
That he cut little squares out; evacuated them
from the syrup before it was too late.
That he eventually had to give up, abandon his evacuation plan
and leave the rest of the village.
I want to skip to the good part, the moment when he looks up.
I don't have the patience to describe her skin
as the exact feeling of a sinking summer sun.
That she was reading a paper and looked up too and smiled briefly.

Or maybe it isn't my impatience but knowing that every story
is ultimately a tragedy. That a happy ending just means that
you don't know the ending. That even comedies
are tragedies, just really funny tragedies.
In pop fiction there is always a happy ending.

After the bad Vampire/ Pirate Lord/ Warlock is finally killed
the hero still has to go home to a dysfunctional marriage
and a drug problem. Still has to find a way to pay the rent.
The beautiful, captured woman now set free,
still has to go home to her two kids and food stamps,
still has to deal with her post traumatic stress disorder
and drug problem.

So maybe I just want to skip to that real ending, where he looks up
and sees her, maybe reading a paper. She looks up and sees a jar
on a table in the corner. The end of the story
where, for a moment, he is in love with a strange woman
and she is in love with a jar of chrysanthemums. Or maybe
it is just the fluidity of the poem. That it is so quickly changed.
In this poem maybe he does not look up first. She looks up
from the real estate offerings because she needs to get out of her apartment
immediately and sees him tapping a straw from its sleeve on the table.
The end of the story where, for a moment, she is in love with a strange man
and he is in love with the stack of pancakes headed for his table.

Evolution

Assignment in a Senior Seminar Dec. 07:
   "Write an essay that describes your intellectual
   evolution over the course of the semester."

At first start of class.
Me am be opening can with rock. Rock I steal
from witch in cave next door.
It magic rock.

After the second week I purchase can opener.
I purchase at place you call Maaallll.

Now of course, nearing the end of the semester
I have adopted many
new practices and customs. Now I wear Chinos, drink
Macchiato, and enjoy a good pedicure
when I can spare an hour. I subscribe
to many scientific journals and find the writings
of Friedrich Nietzsche trés trés magnifique.

If any, doubt, the profound
effect that your inestimable teachings
has had on this student's cranial development;
or the power of your Ph.D. to mend the ignorant,

I crush skull with rock.

It magic.

A Plea for Leniency

Mostly, Damien is a bastard.
It doesn't bother him,
the lines that will encompass his face.
His hair turned gray.
The rest of him may deserve that.
But his hands do not.

Those hands have plucked
a single apple blossom without crushing it.
They have held a baby, fingers
cradling the soft head.
Then laid her back down
without a mark on the skin.

They have held a hot iron skillet steady,
added oil and eggs, whisked them into the rice.
They felt more at home resting
unobtrusively in his pockets.

They weren't responsible for that boy's nose.
They did not know what they wanted
when they took that money
from his neighbor's dresser.

These hands do not deserve to be old.

They have only ever done what he told them.

Dogs I Owned in a Dream I Had

The dogs are white Border collies,
but someone has spray painted them
blue, green, reddish silver. One of them has a Mohawk,
which makes me think,
he must be into punk rock,
the guy whose dream they emigrated from, not the dog.
Though maybe the dog likes punk rock too.

Their claws are clicking down the hall.
The dogs are ready,
same battle every night, attack and defend.
I pull the sheets over my head,
and kick at their heads,
until they are curled up on the covers.
I stretch, they growl.
I pull on the covers, they growl.
I growl for them to let me sleep, to go back
to whatever punk rock bastard first dreamt them,
they have no comment.

They sleep between me and the wall.
As if I will protect them from the monster
in the closet, called work clothes.
They follow me to the door every morning.

After I am gone they crouch at the top of the stairs
bark, and bark, and bark,
at strangers, the front window,
the television,
a box on the floor,
any imaginary damn thing.
They sort the trash from the bag in the kitchen,
delicious, or delicious.
Chew on the pile of broken sticks
that used to be a rocking chair.

After the paper is in pieces they nod their heads.
Slurp from the toilet.
It's like boat drinks and tether ball around here,
stupid, punk-rock-dog heaven.

They hear the key puncture, the deadbolt
jerked from the frame. Their feet inch closer to the door,
forgetting the exact distance.
The yelp of smashed toe is wholly gratifying.

I drag my tail into the soft leather chair.
Just want to gnaw on a bottle of scotch.
To sort the bills from the mailbox,
overdue or overdue.
Chew on the bundle of broken sticks
that used to be a life.

The dog without the Mohawk, which I believe

to have sustained fewer head traumas, will yo-yo

his nose under my hand, force me up from that one point.

The other dog,

blue Mohawk dog,

will run in little circles

like some spastic satellite, circling his tail.

Then skip to the back door.

It isn't fair

them teaming up like this.

But they are young.

So I drink on the back porch,

whip a slick green ball into empty space.

How Water Protects Us

In the beginning Fire was free
to sit on the couch, drink vodka,
smoke and burn holes in the carpet.
His anger would smolder all day.
By the time Water got back
to the house Fire would shout,
"I need more fuel," shake
the empty bottles. He thought it clever.
Fire wanted someone to blame
for all his failures. Why he never burned
down a whole forest.
Why he never made the five o'clock news.
Fire always wanted to be a star.

It only took a little spark.
When Fire got drunk, or depressed,
or worried that Water would run
or had friends or talked about him
Fire's anger would flare up.
He'd pull Water by her long hair,
sometimes tearing it out.
He'd choke her, hit her,
blacken Water's arms, back, face.
Water would cry and cry and cry whole rivers.

One night while Fire was asleep
Water was still awake, her bruises
and burns kept her awake, her fear.
That night she pressed a pillow
over his face to smother him.

Water dug a deep hole in her backyard,
hid Fire in it and shoveled dirt onto him.
Now water could go where she wanted
and she went everywhere. But Fire
was not dead, he is still there, embers
in that deep hole. And sometimes,
sometimes, he tries to escape.
He will stick his head out and stretch
his arms, and burn everything he touches
until he runs into Water, who puts him back
in his hole. Fire is afraid of her and she protects us.

Kate Poems

At Dirty Dick's and Sloppy Joe's
We drank our Liquor straight,
Some went upstairs with Margery,
and some alas with Kate...
— Auden

I   Alas with Kate

The rose weaving up to kiss the base of the ship at her elbow,
the ship sailing on a breaker that curves to the soft bitable hollow
at the bend in her arm, how that sea supports
the delicate chartreuse scales of the mermaid hiding her breasts
behind her arm and waving to sailors to come a little bit
closer and how the mystery of her face disappears up a sleeve
on Kate's robe, her Forget-me-not robe,
and if a wind manages to sneak in the door of this place,
if it manages to make it past the tables of sailors
and survives the thick haze of smoke, if it manages to
crawl its way far enough to caress that robe how, being stirred by that breeze
the robe reminds the poet of the sea and he wonders
if this were purposeful, catering as Kate did, largely to sailors
and how, past the blue folds, another tattoo, a serpent,
its emerald head resting on an apple, weaves around her throat
and down into the glistening darkness between

Kate's breasts and that is where the knowledge
of her tattoos end for him because he has never asked
or spoken but watched and twisted his hands
on the glass of warm liquor in front of him,
pressing his teeth into his teeth as some rough whaler
places a hand on her arm, her back, her rump and pulls her
toward the staircase at the back of the bar that leads
upstairs to her small room where he has caught a glimpse
from his table as Kate and her newly paid sailor sashay into the room
of the tiny camisole on the wall over the table with the jar
holding a few sprigs of Butterflyweed and those two items
of comfort hint that night after night the poet will stare
back down at his drink and his next drink until Kate
comes back down, instead of tossing on his coat
and slamming the door to the bar behind him and return
to writing or at least to a new bar where he could at least breathe
and talk and not stare at the hint of a tail, on each ankle, a carp
and a dolphin as they disappear into the waters of her robe.

II   Alas, said Kate,

Who woke from dreaming. Scything arms
Were pulling her under the ship's prow.
Above, the mermaid's steady eyes
Unblinking in the nauseating
Up and down. Obscenely round
Breasts poorly covered by forearm. Kate's

Hands cupping uselessly. The sea
Encloses. Briny water stings
Her nose and throat, and sinking fingers
Slide past the mermaid's slippery scales.

Alas, said Kate, who shook her dream
From shoulders like a robe and, sitting
Up in bed, decided this
Would be a day for gathering
More Butterflyweed. Her dreams still coming
In splashes, she rubbed her chest as if
To smear her snake tattoo. Night's work
Was hours off, so she dressed with care
And pinned her hair. She lingered at
The looking glass and swallowed hard.

Alas, said Kate, descending the stairs.
The pub's ammonia-morning-after
Stench lay visibly on clouds
Of pipe smoke, tiered throughout the room.
The visceral reality
Of her profession struck her like
The wooden tail from last night's dream.
She turned, but saw a man asleep
Beside his glass. Kate lifted his wallet,
Ran her fingers through his hair,
And vanished out the door.

An Entirely True Story

for Autumn Newman

"We have to save it!" She jumped into the lake to save a baby
killer whale from drowning. I explained to her that whales don't drown.
"They can stay under water for like, 20 minutes."
But she was already waist deep.
I tried to explain that this lake freezes
solid in the winter, that it was only 30 yards across,
that it was too small to hold a pod of orca,
it could not sustain a sufficient food source.
I tried to explain that it was a fresh water lake,
that it wasn't even a real lake but a reservoir
made in the seventies and before that it was just a valley.
But she had cut the fishing lines it was wrapped in and peeled the porpoise
out of the muddy suction of the lake bottom.
I tried to explain that no orca lived in Horsetooth reservoir,
no orca live in any lakes anywhere.
But she had already dragged one-half of a white-wall tire onto the shore.
I tried to tell her it was a tire. That it had Goodyear written on the side.
I tried to tell her that if it were an orca
the last thing it would need is to be pulled onto shore
and hit repeatedly on the back, that there are no federal guidelines
for mouth to blowhole resuscitation and she might be doing more harm
than good.

But she kept breathing into the hole in the tire, pausing on occasion to cry a little and repeat "If we had only been sooner."
I tried to tell her it was ok, that it was too late,
that there was nothing else she could do.
But Autumn took the tire back to the water and gave it a little push.
Truthfully, it swam away.

Spring Chores

First, the air conditioner needs to be installed in the upstairs window. And everyone's drunk of course, and an asshole. Taking down the vertical blinds is the first step, but one of the end caps broke and I angle the thing so all the blinds fall out. So the first step of third floor air conditioner repair is to fix the blinds. But I slice my hand up trying to force the small plastic sliders into the sharp metal bar and begin hammering them into place with a wrench, which breaks them all and now they won't slide or rotate which is fine with me because I am never in this room. Then we drop the screws out the window and since we started this project after nine-thirty at night we cannot find them in the mulch three stories below us. But we all decide we don't really need those screws anyway. So we cuss the air conditioner up to the window and slam it closed. I'm sure it is plenty secure but to double check we nail the window shut. It will be fine.

In the garage the recyclables are the first to go. One truck-load dispersed to nine different locations because Rocky Recycling takes paper but only certain types of paper and not aluminum or plastic and Best Stop takes phone books and the grocery store takes aluminum cans and Mountain Maintenance takes glass bottles and the plastic are split between the place north of town and the place south of town and we can't find anywhere to take batteries so we put them back in the garage. We used to leave the recyclables on the curb but we learned that all recyclables went straight to the landfill, as it was more cost effective, though they keep leaving us recycle bins.

Then we move the workout gear from one side of the garage to the other then back again, which is actually quite heavy. I think this is the first time anyone has gotten a workout from it. Then we sort the antique bear traps which were here when we moved in which I am forbidden from ever touching again or setting up in the front yard. So someone else sorts them by amount of rust and hangs them back on the wall. Chairs are stacked, tools placed into a much neater haphazard pile on the floor, the floor is swept and the brooms are all thrown out for being dirty, and someone tells me about the hantavirus and how you get it from being around mouse droppings so I spray the entire garage with chlorine and lie on the driveway positive of a quick death. In the future I wish people would tell me about life threatening illnesses ahead of time or not at all. Then we plant sunflowers by moonlight, smoke cigarettes in the garden, pass out.

We'll Need a Cartoon Mascot

Final in Business 305, Dec. 07:
   "Design a new theme park, pick a location
   and create a sales pitch."

We need new, exciting theme parks.
The future is Three Mile Island
and Love Canal. We could buy them
for a steal. Picture a rollercoaster
that goes through the reactor,
it would already come with a light show.
A waterslide log ride through the canal.

The gift shops would make a fortune.
We could sell Geiger counters,
lead glasses. Make a brand
new energy drink, bright green,
packaged in tiny yellow barrels,
called SLUDGE ©. We'll put warnings
on the label. Guaranteed
to be banned from all schools
and federal buildings for causing heart
palpitations which will boost sales.
Tastes great with licorice-flavored liqueur.
Served chilled, grade school kids will love it.

Then make a citrus flavor called OOZE ©.

We could run daily, mandatory tours.

All led by impotent,

cancer-ridden,

flipper babies.

It could be real heartwarming.

They could work for tips.

They couldn't run away.

A Little Service Please

The car idling in the back of the parking lot?
I am not going to stereotype and say it is
waiting for drugs because they could be
waiting on a dog breeder to meet them
with a new puppy but statistically speaking
they are far more likely to be waiting
on their drug dealer than their Labradoodle dealer.
Drug dealers are pretty inconsiderate.
They expect you to be wherever on time and frequently
in a less than savory neighborhood but they
can take as long as they want. They only deal in cash
and sometimes you don't always feel like hitting the ATM
before waiting in a parked car in an empty parking lot
for hours. They are the least punctual people on earth
and that is just not a successful business model.
I wish that drug dealers could be a little more considerate,
act like a real business, offer coupons, two for one
Labor Day specials. C'mon down and get half-off
four grams of mushrooms with the purchase
of one oz. of premium grade grass.
We are practically giving them away cuz' we're crazy
down at Crazy Phil's Altered States Emporium, remember
no matter what state you live in you don't have to
live in a state of sobriety. I personally quit doing drugs

just to teach drug dealers a lesson in customer service and encourage others to do so too.

Plus, to be honest, some of them are criminals.

Ignorance Always Thinks It Knows Best Because It Doesn't Know Any Better

I want to start a poem in a room
I don't own in a city I haven't been
to. This poem would start, I am sick
of the snow. Aren't you sick of the snow?
It's ugly and it's everywhere, old
mop water and sewage, shaken out
on the ground in this new ugly hide.
But there is no snow. I have not seen snow
this year. The ski resorts are worried,
they rented every snow cone machine
in the country and turned them on
full blast so the mountains really are purple.
The snowboarders are pissed.
But all the people at my brother's work
don't believe in global warming
and say they have to reeducate their kids
when they get home from school.
If it were me, I would choose a different word
than reeducation since it is creepy and vaguely
threatening, but that is what they do,
reeducate their children, in small dungeons
in the basement, singing hosannas
and dousing them with buckets of water,

or at least that is how I assume it works,

having never reeducated anyone myself.

But whether or not all the little reeducation camps

in the world tell all their children

there is no such thing as global warming

or that the earth is flat and the sun

revolves around it and there were

no such things as dinosaurs or extinction,

it does not change the fact that I have not

seen a single lick of snow all year

and it is preventing me from writing

my poem about how sick of it I am

and how lonely I feel in the middle

of a great lake of snow. A lot of mosquitoes though.

Hard to feel lonely in a room full of mosquitoes,

you are always the most popular person there.

Before the War of the Asphodels

1.

I forgive you
after all
I should be pleased
at least

you are eating
fruit finally
a good example
for your patients

I hope they do
not resort to theft
though I don't
mean to scold

2.

I have broken
your grandmother's
antique cup
but at least I didn't

leave the shards
on the floor for
your bare feet
to find forgive me

but I never
liked it anyway
so ugly
and so old

3.

I have taken
the money
that was in
the sock drawer

and which
I know you were
saving for new
golf clubs

I bought new
bone china
a floral pattern
edged in gold

4.

I have replaced
the plums
that I so senselessly
ate thinking

wrongly that
food in the icebox
was for eating
but now there

is a bushel
of plums so make
your jam quick
before they all mold

What I Got

I've got three-thousand dollars in a bank account
which doesn't belong to me. I've got
sixty-thousand dollars in debt which does
belong to me. I've got no health insurance,
but neither does anyone else I know.
I quit a job that I hated and didn't pay me
enough and now I have a job that I like
that pays even less. I've got thirteen dollars,
which does actually belong to me so
I can buy a twelve pack of beer for my brother and me.
I've got a car which isn't that bad, a clock radio
that sets itself, two lamps, a small TV, a stereo
which won't play tapes anymore
but still plays CDs which is fine
because I don't have any tapes any more.
I've got seventeen CDs, I had nineteen,
Bob Marley and Sublime got stolen.
I've bought those CDs four times
and they keep getting stolen. I think they might be
the most stolen CDs ever. I try to listen
to stuff that never got regular airplay
so they won't be stolen. I like this Gypsy punk rock band
and had that CD, until I played it for a friend. He liked it
so much he stole it. I would call my friend a dick

and demand my CD back but he's crazy,
he's cut a few guys in bar fights with a box cutter.
I still listen to a lot of Bob Dylan which reminds me
of a friend I had who really liked Dylan.
He went into renal failure after too much Tylenol,
was in the hospital for eight or nine days.
By the second day the hospital had a new liver for him
but didn't operate. Then they had a second liver,
because it was like, a holiday weekend
and there seem to be plenty of available organs
over a long weekend but they didn't give him that liver either
and he died. He didn't have health insurance
and the doctors don't want to waste their time
handing out livers to people who can't pay for them.
But they still charged my friend's family
for the dialysis unit and the hospital stay,
and what is that about, shouldn't there be a kind of warranty,
like buying a dishwasher, if it doesn't work,
if the patient still dies, then I get my money back.
Doctors, all that talk about wanting to help people
is a pack of lies so fuck 'em.
The man who performed the ceremony
spoke in Navajo I believe. He played a wooden flute,
sounded like crying. At the grave he said
his people believe that a wind was like an animal,
snatched the soul up with its teeth, carried it off
to the afterlife. As he said this, a cold beast of wind

coyoteed through the cemetery, shaking trees, throwing dust,
then sped off, heading west. My friend's family just sat there,
stared straight ahead, like they couldn't hear it.
If you looked around though, all the crackers,
such as myself, pointed eyes at each other.
We didn't believe in the wind. We still don't believe
in the wind. Do not mention it again. After the funeral,
everybody got drunk, that's what we do after every funeral.
I've had a lot of hangovers. I have twenty- nine cents
left over from the beer. I have four beers left
from the twelve pack. I have bad dreams
where I hear the wind. I have bad dreams
where no one has health insurance, but I already said
nobody has health insurance. I have bad dreams about the wind.

My Cancer Hogs the Covers

The first thing everyone asks about is the hair.
A woman can't hide it if the hair goes,
it's a neon avalanche started by the word sick.

Well you could always say you asked the stylist
for a little off the top and she didn't
speaka de angleesh asoa goot.

It is easier to ask then the other question.
Are you going to die? Though that is what
everyone whispers behind their teeth.

When my mother told me
she had cancer, she was forty-three.

You see a lot of teeth around a cancer patient.
Everyone comes around with these sad smiles,
quietly smiling and hugging everyone in the room.
Taking long looks at the cancer-ee like they can see it,
a stain spreading across the floor.

When I learned I had cancer I shaved my head.
I expected to lose it anyway.
That is what most people think,

started with the old male pattern, decided to run.
I can always wear a fedora,
lymphoma into fashion.

I named my cancer Phil.
He is an unwelcome house guest,
keeps me up all night, never pays for food,
won't leave.

I'm just kidding. I don't have cancer
but it runs in the family and I smoke a lot.
I want to have my cancer poem ready for when I need it.
I want something clever and I'm not
sure I could escape the maudlin later on.

My cancer will not be a pair of handcuffs,
a hat with nothing in it.
More like the last trick in the magic show,
a puff of smoke,

Way Over Here,

and when you look back
I'll already be gone.

To Devan's Daughter

You may wonder about this letter
and why it is attached to this jar.
I am a friend of your mother. Actually
your grandparents were my best friends.
I've known your mother since she was a baby.
The jar contains honey. I left you
this because all the bees are gone now.
This could be one of the last jars of honey too
so it might be worth a lot of money.
There will never be another jar
of honey. You may not believe this
but your grandmother was afraid of bees
so if you see one in a museum, try to
imagine her running in circles around it
screaming. While you are at the museum
look at the butterflies. They were wonderful,
all stained glass sailboaty, tossing around
on the waves of a light breeze. You may wonder
what it was like to have one sit on your finger,
though you do not believe your grandmother
and her stories of how they did. Believe
that children used to catch them and tear
their wings off. I don't think this
is what led to their extinction but it probably didn't

help. Since the bees and butterflies are all gone
there are no longer any pollinators left.
Which is the reason you have never tasted
a strawberry or a pecan. No pears or peaches,
cranberry, cherry or plum. They were delicious.
It started in 2005. Millions of bees
just disappeared. They called it CCD,
Collapsed Colony Disease.
There were a lot of theories. Pesticides,
hormones, a new virus. One scientist
said it was all the cell phones, I say physics
finally caught up to them because I don't
like to admit that it was our fault.
Every third bite of food was pollinated by bees.
I have left you this last jar of honey
because something terrible will happen to you.
Perhaps your parents die from the prevalent
cancers or respiratory diseases, I don't know.
But one day you will be so sad
you think your throat is being crushed. You will
need cheering up and nothing will work
and you will already be drunk.
Open this jar. Look out your door at the horrible
brown sky, and you will know
what sunshine once tasted like,
which is one more thing we wasted,
one more thing we used to have.

DAMIEN SHUCK received an MFA from the University of Southern Maine. Poems in this collection have appeared previously in *Cider Press Review, Occupoetry, Shimmyhoots Review,* and *Stonecoast Lines.*

www.ingramcontent.com/pod-product-compliance
Lightning Source LLC
LaVergne TN
LVHW041342080426
835512LV00006B/579